Whispers of another realm

Karis Lee

BookLeaf
Publishing

India | USA | UK

Presentation by *BookLeaf Publishing*

Web: www.bookleafpub.com

E-mail: info@bookleafpub.com

ISBN: 9789363305892

First edition 2024

I extend my heartfelt thanks to my Junior Year
English teacher, whose guidance was like a
beacon in a world of stories, and to the many
authors whose fantastical realms have fueled
my imagination and guided my quest. My
deepest gratitude also goes to my parents,
whose unwavering support has been a steadfast
enchantment, allowing me to follow my dreams
through every adventure and challenge. Your
belief in my journey has been my greatest
magic

Just another Romeo and Juliet story

I wandered around an unusual place
With millions of stars implanted in space
I saw a mountain up ahead
With bright city lights beneath the bed

There was a whisper, a voice, a song
"The land where dreams belong"
Was all I heard
Everything else was a blur

I ran along the gray cobblestones of the city
Through the serenity
Searching for the owner of the voice
Amongst the noise

And there he was
In the amidst of the buzz
Standing there, almost as if he was waiting
Waiting for me

But alas the book closes
Like the Red Sea by Moses
And I face reality
Going back to brutality

Our story is just like Romeo and Juliet
….Fictional

My first heartbreak

I sense the end approaching as our bond is
fading
From my friend to love it all was cascading

I guess that's the price I must bear
After finishing you in a day, without a care
Now closing the book, without a second glance
Leaving behind our fleeting romance

I'll bid you farewell
My first heartbreak, so surreal
From a man in my book, our story untold
But in my heart, forever you'll hold

Wings

She was a girl who used to dance with the stars
Even landing on Mars
But now all she can do is dream
After all…the world clipped her wings

Still searching

I'm still searching for that world
I can see it in my dreams
But when I wake up it's gone

I'm still searching for that world
In that world there still is good and bad
But in that world instead of fighting for a spot in
college with knowledge, you fight a war with
swords and magic.

I'm still searching for that world
The world that appears when I close my eyes
But that world doesn't seem to be searching for
me…

Power

The greatest power you hold is deciding what
breaks you

Hate

I hate it when you give me butterflies
Even worse when you make me kick my feet as
I read

I hate it when you're not around and the fact that
you left me alone after the book closed

But mostly, I hate the way I don't hate you, not
even close, not even a little bit, not even at all.
In fact I love you for bringing light into my life
with words and sentences.

Magic on a shelf

The ink floats around,
The words whisper in grace,
Woven tales and dreams abound,
In a boundless, timeless space

The climax awaiting me in just a moment,
As I travel throughout the magic,
Each page a world where dreams are potent,
Unfolding wonders, pure and tragic

Yet here they rest, a quiet shelf,
The ink and stories, still and mute,
A treasure trove of worlds untold,
In a book where dreams take root

The heart of a villain

In lands where dragons' shadows loom,
Where magic's breath and darkness bloom,
A hero stands with sword in hand,
To save the world, a tragic plan.

He slays the one he loves the most,
A sacrifice for the greater boast,
With tears that fall like rain from skies,
He hopes the world will never realize.

Yet in the dark, a villain's plight,
Who'd shatter realms to make things right,
To save the one he holds so dear,
He'd sacrifice the world's last tear.

In fantasy's great woven weave,
Heroes and villains both deceive,
For in their hearts, the lines are blurred,
By love and fate, their choices stirred.

The hero's blood may seal the fate,
Of countless lives in a world so great,
While villains' hands may forge the night,
To keep a single soul in light.

Be Real, not Perfect

"Be real, not perfect," he whispered low,
In a realm where such truths could freely flow.
Here, I am told I'm enough as I am,
Yet I must return to a world that's a sham.

Back to the realm where they urge me to blend,
To fit in with ease, where doubts never end.
As the book closes gently, I know it's time,
To leave this truth behind and face the climb

SHUT UP

Make it stop,
MAKE IT STOP,
the world spins on, an endless whirl,
The voices rise in harsh, cruel swirl:
"SUCH A DISAPPOINTMENT,"
"A FAILURE."
SHUT UP!
"YOU'LL NEVER BE GOOD ENOUGH."
SHUT UP,
SHUT UP,
SHUT UP.

Yet through the clamor, faint and small,
A tiny voice cuts through it all:
"Are you okay?"

I look up to see the owners of the voices,
and…it's me.
But the tiny voice that whispers soft and free
Turns out to be a book, a quiet plea

Thank you

To the books where we escape...
....And the authors that write it

Liam Mairi

I could hear the crack in my heart
As he let out his final breathe, saying "it's been
my honor"
The next scenes blurred, words jumbled and lost,
Until I realized my tears had caused the gloss.

My story

For once....I would like to have my story told instead of being the teller....

Growth

I'm not as fierce as Nesta Archeron,Nor as
renowned as Sophie Foster,Or as astute as Alex
Bailey.

Perhaps that's why I'm still waiting—
Waiting for a world of wonders and magic,
Just as they did

Yet, Nesta wasn't always strong,
Sophie wasn't always celebrated,
And Alex wasn't always socially wise.
But they grew,
And so shall I

Life story (six-word memoir)

Chased Dreams In Enchanted Forests, Grew Wiser

Both story's must be heard

Villains will remain villains if only the hero's tale is told

Luna and Soleil

Once upon a time,
There was a moon named Luna, wedded to the
sun, Soleil.
Luna would often request Soleil's light to shine
brightly in the night,
And Soleil, with a cold yet polite nod, would
grant her wish without asking for anything in
return.

Though Soleil seemed distant and unfeeling,
Luna understood his true nature;
For occasionally, Soleil would ask for a hug.
So, every hundred years, Luna embraced this
rare request,
Turning it into a cherished tradition she called
"The Eclipse."

There's always another tale

You may be the hero in someone's story, a
beacon of hope and courage
But remember, in another tale
You might always be cast as the villain,
embodying the shadows and trials that others
face

Luna and Soleil

Once upon a time,
There was a moon named Luna and a sun named Soleil. Luna frequently asked Soleil to light up the night sky, and Soleil, with a distant nod, complied without asking for anything in return.

Yet Luna understood Soleil's true nature. Every century, Soleil longed for a hug. So, Luna secretly established a tradition: every hundred years, during the eclipse, she would embrace Soleil, calling it "the eclipse."

29.5 days

Guess what! I found another woman who has her period much worse—the moon. She endures her cycle every month for 29.5 days

If the weather can cry, why can't you?

Why do you like rainy days?
Because they remind us that even the weathers
allowed to cry

www.ingramcontent.com/pod-product-compliance
Lightning Source LLC
La Vergne TN
LVHW050304200726
843509LV00015B/3148